LEADERSHIP DEVELOPMENT:
# IF STEVE JOBS WAS COACHING YOU

-

Charismatic Leadership Lessons
Borrowed from Steve Jobs
for High Potential People and Leaders.

*- The Leadership Series -*

# - Life Hacks Books –

Easy-to-read books
to do better and feel better

# ABOUT
# 'THE LEADERSHIP SERIES'.

The Leadership Series are written with the aim of solving important problems that every single entrepreneur or manager faces one day or another, sooner or later. Only, most people do not seek to address those problems. You apparently are on the way to solving one problem, congratulations!

It will provide you with simple but very relevant and efficient leadership-related solutions that can be used immediately, after a quick read.

The rest will be for you to do!

Take action!

# WARNING:

This book has been written for motivated entrepreneurs and fast growing SME business owners willing to become better leaders, passionate C-level persons interested in leadership, and success-focused people. It is not suitable for couch potatoes, "I know, I know!" people or low potential and defeat-oriented persons. Just saying…

This book has been edited with the contribution of Philippe Bonnet, APAC Manager at Business Talents, a professional business & leadership coaching group based in Hong Kong which helps international leaders and entrepreneurs operating in Asia to deal with their leadership and management routine on a daily basis. Philippe is also the Founder of the Business Talents Network [BTN] club, one of Hong Kong's striving networking group. Don't we all want to improve our business?

* * * *

# IN THIS BOOK:

# INTRODUCTION

Steve Jobs co-founded Apple in 1976 with Steve Wozniak. Both had the exceptional ambition to bring computers into every home. Forty years later, computers are indeed in every home, the Apple ones in particular, not to forget those we carry in our pockets, jackets or handbags on a daily and hourly basis.

But beyond this business success is a fascinating leadership story that numerous articles and comments have tried to analyze. In most of them, the question is always the same: whether or not Steve Jobs was a good leader and how he actually managed products, people and business developments throughout his career.

Still, one question remains unanswered for: HOW COULD THINGS WORK FOR YOU IF STEVE JOBS WAS COACHING YOU?

This book focuses on this exact question. One, it will give you an opportunity to think about a variety of ideas and issues related to the many skills and difficulties that have been characteristic of Steve Jobs' leadership. Two, it will help you think about how you could apply this pattern of thinking to your own business needs.

The book offers a comprehensive review of the ten major challenges faced by most entrepreneurs nowadays. All in all, this book offers about thirty-five leadership tips that can be borrowed from Jobs' life and experience and applied immediately to your own leadership methods.

At the end of each session, of course, a series of questions is provided to help you think further and improve your leadership by applying the discussions to your own management style. It's up to you now…

# LEADERSHIP LESSON #1: HAVE THE RIGHT MOTIVATIONS

The first - and perhaps the most important and decisive – factor when it comes to leading a team or a project is motivation. Your motivation. Your motivations. Your teams' motivations.

Your motivations have an enormous impact on the success of your undertakings! If your main goal is merely to make cash for yourself at the end of the year (for instance), you will have troubles achieving results because you will be on your own. If you are not motivated by making the most of everything, similarly, your leadership will suffer.

Now, the leadership methods applied by Steve Jobs suggest the following: having the right motivations intrinsically relates to passion and requires leaders to have a permanently positive attitude.

**The right motivations are passion-related.** As basic as it sounds, nobody will work to just make *you* earn more money. They will need more than this and *your* motivations must therefore take into account the other stakeholders' needs and aspirations!

To be even clearer, your motivations as a leader must have a lot to do with passions. If you are passionate about your work and goals, your team will feel and relate to your passion, they will make your goals theirs and will help you reach the impossible.

Steve Jobs knew this very well and made it a key element of his leadership method. In fact, one

18

of the quotes that often comes up on the Internet when doing research on Steve Jobs' leadership methods refers to a speech to his staff in which he insisted on the idea that the first motivation for a well-done job must always start from passion, because people with passion can change the world for the better!

So, if Steve Jobs was coaching you, chances are that he would push you to make sure you are moved by your passions rather than by money or personal ambitions. In other words, do what you are the best at doing, and do it because you sincerely enjoy doing it. Believe in your products and be passionate about the way you talk about them, show their tremendous potential and give your team an excellent reason to believe in the products so that they can work hard(er) to promote them too.

For example, if you are good at explaining things, teach your team how to progress and do better, then they will achieve greater results! If you are good at making people feel better, add a dose of encouragement and support to your leadership and your team will feel considered and pushed forward! If you are good with numbers more than with interpersonal skills, use the numbers to show your team the potential and let them make the most of their passions and personal skills to reach the goals!

In any case, let passion do the job.

**Having the right motivations deeply relates to positive-thinking.** The positive attitude is a very important aspect of leadership and works in pair with motivations. And passion. We'll see later in this book that Steve Jobs was very demanding and even hard at times with his staff, but he was nonetheless always positive in both his management style and life style.

From a management perspective, he was convinced that positive-thinking was the best way forward and therefore he always made sure that his staff aimed for success. From a personal perspective, and particularly as an adopted child, resentment had little importance to him and, in truth, he never allowed difficulties to take over his ambitions, passions and motivations. Moving forward and thinking positively was more relevant, important and efficient.

The lesson here is that you should embrace the positive attitude. Give importance to whatever moves you, allow yourself to make the most of people and developments of all sorts, capitalize on what is good and positive but banish resentment and problems from your management style and leadership. Your personal vision will only improve if you provide your staff with 'half-full glass' ways of thinking and leave 'half-empty' logics far behind, and the perception that your team has of you will significantly improve too!

## Now, what are *your* motivations?

Let's use your imagination for a minute or two. Think. If you could actually have a discussion with Steve Jobs regarding your own leadership skills, how would you answer the following questions? No rush, take your time and write down your conclusions and feelings. Please note, however, that writing is the first step. You will then need to re-think your methods and apply your conclusions to your own methods. Ready?

Are you driven by money, power and results?

Is your leadership reflecting your motivations?

What room do you leave for passion in your leadership and work methods?

To what extent do you manage to motivate and engage your teams and partners and to what extent do you think your motivations help in doing this? Could you achieve more by reviewing your motivations and adapting your leadership to take into account your teams' motivations?

Oh, and of course, have you ever thought about adding a dose of positive-thinking to your leadership style and life?

# LEADERSHIP LESSON #2:
# THE VISION IS ON YOU

A second key pillar of Steve Jobs' leadership was the ability to develop a vision that his staff was not only *able* to follow but *happy* to follow. While passion can you get somewhere, it is your vision that will eventually determine where passion will lead you. In other words, the responsibility to determine the project's vision that all your team and partners will follow is on YOU.

**Working on the vision is about setting the direction that motivated people will follow.** Steve Jobs saw passion as the way forward, but his vision or ultimate goal when he created Apple was to make computers accessible to everyone. Let me repeat. His vision was not to build computers which at the time were not meant for the mass: his vision was that sooner or later anyone would be able to use a computer in their everyday life.

Whether they are staff members, partners or customers, the people who make part of your business project need something to agree with, something to adhere to, follow and promote. Hence, your job as a leader is not to set 'a' direction, you must imagine, clarify and promote 'the' direction that will become everyone else's rule.

**Building a vision requires a real ability to anticipate.** The logical continuity of the previous idea is that you, as a leader, must develop your ability to anticipate. And there are lots to anticipate! Trends, developments,

26

evolutions, not to mention news that do not exist yet.

Steve Jobs' vision that people would at some point all use computers routinely was largely about anticipating markets that did not exist at the time.

The same leadership skills applied for a variety of products that have over time made Apple's success. For instance, Ipods were never necessary (other portable music devices were available) but he saw a market for them that would also allow creating additional markets for on-demand-music (iTunes) which significantly changed our lives and even more drastically impacted the disc industry over the past decades.

The same logic of course worked for Iphones, Ipads or Apple TV solutions which have overtime reshuffled the cards of technological progress in ways that no competitors even thought possible at the time, and allow us to use technology on a daily basis.

So, while vision is essential, it is nothing without

27

anticipation, which means that you must integrate an important dose of revolutionary thinking into your leadership methods. This obviously applies to the development of new products, but the rule also works when it comes to finding new ways of motivating or managing people. What works today for your staff might not work eternally, therefore you need to do some serious forward thinking here as well to anticipate your team's needs.

**Anticipation methods are important.** Steve Jobs had certain rules when it came to anticipating and organizing efforts. Particularly in relation to meetings and brainstorming sessions.

Chances are that you are thinking about organizing an anticipation brainstorming session or focus group on Monday, but wait a minute. Apple's Founder was very demanding and had some precise ideas about what worked and what didn't.

In particular, and in contrast with the market testing methods widely promoted in business courses and business books, Jobs was known for having no interest and no patience for focus groups, which he tended to consider as irrelevant. For him, anticipation was about creating new demand and markets, therefore consumers with little technical know-how and expertise were incapable of offering any views on the future of an industry.

For Jobs, instead, they had to be surprised with innovation they would not only want but *need*. Period! In fact, Jobs is often quoted for a reference he made to Henry Ford, who once said that if he had followed his customers' requests, he would have produced faster horses more than car prototypes.

This means that Steve Jobs' leadership was about originality, instinct and guts – forgive my French – more than about permanent feedback and back-and-forth consultations. In other words? Do not merely anticipate, do it well and follow your intuitions.

**Scrambling the eggs also makes part of the anticipation work.** When Jobs created Ipods capable of storing tons of songs and developed the idea of digitally stored and sold music contents with Itunes, he went literally against the market.

As a reminder, the market at the time was still shifting from tapes into new technologies, while the mp3 technology was somehow competing with alternative technologies in the form of hybrid discs capable of replacing CDs while storing more music. A major impact of this innovation, clearly, was also that by transforming the industry Jobs also forced the music majors - which then had no intention to follow and review their economic models – to play by his rules!

Similarly, the Iphone was revolutionary in that it launched a need and demand for smartphones which did not exist at the time. There were literally no applications by then, yet he revolutionized the consumers approach to phones and forced the industry to adapt. The same went, of course, for the Ipad, which then created a need, a demand and a market for tablets of all sorts and sizes.

Hence, Jobs' innovation and leadership scrambled the eggs and forced the whole industry to review their models, their standards, and ultimately to adapt to new developments he initiated without a warning.

## Now, what is <u>your</u> vision like?

Let's keep playing and thinking. How would you answer those questions if Steve Jobs challenged you on the way you handle vision-related work and challenges? Steve Jobs' answer was clear, he kept anticipating continuously. The vision is on you, your turn to act...

Again, thinking about these points is important but you should discuss them with your partners and collaborators. Now...

What is the current state of your niche market?

How innovative is your vision?

What will this market be like in five to ten years from now?

What innovations will be imposed on your industry?

What will your customers expect?

Will you create those innovations or will you struggle to follow the innovations or others?

How can you reshuffle the cards to stay on top of the competition?

How can you make sure that your team will be there durably to progress with you as new challenges appear?

# LEADERSHIP LESSON #3:
# LEAD AND INSPIRE

The third important pillar of Steve Jobs' leadership was his ability to lead and inspire, and he applied four important rules to his daily work. One was that you need to be the person in charge. A second rule was that setting goals is a priority. A third was that you need to develop an ability to inspire. A fourth rule was about being persistent, always.

**Be the captain, be in charge.** Jobs was known for saying "Don't let the noise of others' opinions drown out your own inner voice". This quote can certainly be applied to the previously mentioned consumer-based approach to business development, but in reality, the idea here is to make sure that there is only one captain in the boat.

Leadership is about making decisions and, while consulting with others is important, only the captain decides what happens next. How many businesses fail routinely because the management team fails to make important decisions? Thousands! So, under Jobs' leadership, decisions only came from one person. Him!

The lesson here is: be the captain, be in charge of the vision, decide on the innovation and lead forward. Chances are, indeed, that while you might find this very logical, you are not really deciding alone in practice. Are you?

**Setting goals on a regular basis [week/ quarter/ year/ decade/ jubilee...] is a key aspect of leadership.** You might have a passion and a vision, but without goals there are *no* directions, *no* benchmarks and *no* way for you to organize a follow-up system!

Hence, Steve Jobs was very keen on setting up short-term and long-term goals alike. Hence, he could ensure that his strategy could evolve in time depending on his markets evolutions, depending on his users' needs and depending on his own beliefs, ideas and intuitions or vision. In other words, long term goals give you the direction and a roadmap while short term goals give you means to implement the strategy.

To be reactive to market evolutions and to assess how well you are doing, you therefore need to set-up benchmarks and, obviously, short-term, medium-term and long-term goals. Think about it, we'll come back to this in a minute.

**Remember that leading forward requires an ability to inspire others**. Goals are not the only thing. While a common argument in business methods, courses and books will teach you how to be a seller, Steve Jobs rather believed in his ability to inspire others.

Of course, it is likely that – as mentioned before – most industry actors reviewed their models to follow Jobs' vision because they didn't have a choice at all.

Nonetheless, Jobs certainly did great at inspiring many, starting with his consumers. In turning his consumers into early adopters and eventually into inspired adepts, Jobs has progressively turned generations of consumers and entrepreneurs alike into followers! Many technologies and apps nowadays are driven by the Apple innovations, millions of businesses not only follow the lead but also made the revolution theirs, thus continuing Jobs' efforts and making is vision an absolute and unquestionable reality.

Have you taken steps to try and inspire?

**Persistence is another skill sharp leaders cannot live without.** Think about it. What unique skill – apart from talent, vision, anticipation and inspiration – could take you from building a computer in a garage to building a worldwide community of users and followers while making you one of the major innovators and business leaders after being fired from your own company?

Persistence! Or Perseverance.

As a reminder, Steve Jobs not only persisted on creating the most innovative tools of our modern world. He also persisted in keeping Apple a striving company. Jobs created Apple in 1976 and was fired from it in 1985 by a CEO he nominated himself. Yet, he took over later and even had another company he built (NeXT) sold to Apple in 1997.

While this seems ironical, the one skill behind those developments was always persistence and the belief – or should I say conviction – that an idea was worth fighting for without limits.

Persistence, or the ability not to give up, is therefore a key aspect of Jobs' leadership and a skill that any leader must acquire and nurture. Of course, no one can prevent discouragement. But perseverant and persistent people all have in common the ability to go past difficulties so as to make their vision a reality. In line with the 'one boat one captain' rule, persistence is about being able to stand for yourself, about making decisions that you, as a leader, deem visionary and fit.

Having said this, let's be careful! Obstinacy is the extreme version of persistence and would become a problem in terms of leadership and reputation. So, are you persistent or obstinate?

**Now, can _you_ inspire?**

Again, take a minute to think. How would you reply to these questions if Steve Jobs asked them as part of a face-to-face meeting?

Are you in charge? Are you _really_ in charge?

Do you take command when it comes to creating the vision and making it happen?

Do you occasionally or regularly face leadership issues involving decision-making needs?

Do you set goals? Your own goals?

Do you listen and take your teams' goals into account when setting yours?

How about short-term, medium-term and long-term goals?

Can you inspire others? How? Have you even tried? What successes have you achieved in this

41

regard?

What steps could you take tomorrow to lead others to follow you and support your undertakings?

If you had to describe yourself, how inspiring would you be?

Are you managing your team so as to achieve numbers and statistics or do you leave room for inspiring and meaningful leadership that allows your staff (and clients) to adhere to your vision, agree to it and make it theirs?


Do you give-up easily? Are you easily discouraged? Are you perseverant / persistent? Obstinate perhaps?

People always have ideas, they start new ideas but usually give-up on them very fast. How could you assess your perseverance levels and your ability to make your ideas become a reality?

Do you give-up easily? Are you easily discouraged? Have you considered persisting and insisting more because an idea is worth it?

# LEADERSHIP LESSON #4:
# LONG-TERM VALUE CREATION

The key to a great idea worth fighting for is to
determine whether this idea creates long-term
value. Here again, Steve Jobs' methods and
experience tells us that great leadership goes in
pair with the idea of creating enormous value
for the end-user. Not consumer, 'end-user'.

**Always create value for the end-user.** Think about it, as mentioned earlier Steve Jobs had one important goal in building Apple: bringing computers into our homes and, eventually, making technology accessible.

Now, what would we do nowadays without computers and smartphones? Steve Jobs has become a business and technology leader because he has created tremendous value for millions and, of course, because the creation of value for his customers was a core component of his leadership method!

In line with the idea that your motivations should not be about making money, the lesson here is that you must make value creation for the end-user a core element of your leadership. The question is not about how they can get you more cash, it is simply about how you can solve a problem for them. Find out how you can help your end-user and you will create value. Period!

**Selling dream is more important than selling products.** Importantly, and to go further, a key aspect of value creation for Steve Jobs related to the idea of selling dream. In other words, the challenge for him was not to merely sell Apple products but to create exceptional user experience that the end-users (and their friends!) would ultimately dream about, thus making the product an absolute must-have.

To some extent, therefore, part of Steve Jobs' leadership embedded the strong belief that customers were not customers but end-users with aspirations. Or, even more clearly, people with dreams who could certainly use some help to realize their dreams.

**Boosting user experience makes part of selling a dream.** This point is obviously a repeat of the previous one, but it is so important that it needs to be mentioned as a specific leadership tip, distinct from the 'selling dream' point.

Remember that for a long time – and still now

47

to some extent – the Apple brand has been associated with excellency for designers and creatives. Nowadays, it is rather associated with ease-of-use and exceptional user experience, not to mention trendiness and coolness.

This means that the dream attached to user experience has changed over time but, clearly, it is the user experience that makes the dream for the end-user. In both cases, in giving experts tools to explore and make the most of their lives, passions and dreams, Steve Jobs' leadership has allowed making the brand a creative's must-have.

**Don't forget customer-service.** Working on user experience without giving attention to customer service is risky.

While boosting end-user experience is probably the best way to make innovation relevant (and visible), Steve Jobs pushed the challenge even further. Customer-service at Apple is simple, . Before you buy a product or whenever you have a problem with your product the customer service will be similar. There is no such things as sales teams piling boxes in the Apple stores all around the world, there are only passionate people creating a connection with fantastic customers and helping them to make the most of their lives.

This point is important because, if included into a brand's DNA, user experience at every level (before and after) has the power of tailoring your brand's reputation. Ignore user experience and your brand will be perceived as cheap even though your product is the best. Invest on it and your brand will be praised as being the best. How is that for corporate DNA and leadership?

**Create long-term and firmly grounded values.** By the same token, this leadership method of course made Apple an extremely profitable brand. But that particular point has to do with the fact that, by focusing on customer experience first, Steve Job's leadership has created a long-term market firmly grounded on robust values that are shared with the end-users, everywhere in the world.

49

In other words, the idea of creating long-term value for your end-users goes in pair with the idea of creating values that your brand and teams will be able to invest on, focus on and capitalize on. When the consumers can tell whether or not a brand has values, their trust in the brand increases. The lack of such values, in contrast, sends the message that the company is not committed and won't stand behind the products and end-users. Quite a difference!

**Now, how do _you_ create value?**

Once again, how would you answer the following questions if you had an opportunity to discuss them with Steve Jobs? Take five minutes, think and revise your position!

Are you selling products to make cash or do you consider value creation as the core aspect of your business?

Are you selling a dream and helping your end-users to realize something important to them?

Is the post-buying customer's experience part of the dream you are selling or could it become a problem?

Finally, are you working on building long-term values that will naturally be associated with your brand by the customer and guarantee a steady flow of revenue in the long run?

# LEADERSHIP LESSON #5:
# CREATE A NEED

Values and dreams were an extremely important part of Steve Jobs' leadership, but the idea of selling dreams comes together with the idea of creating a need that the customer or end-user is not aware of. Not yet anyway.

**Creating a need is key.** Take the Itunes system for example. No competitor existed at the time, and selling the Ipod was directly related to the idea of creating the Itunes platform which would later allow selling on-demand-music to the masses.

So, Steve Jobs and Apple had to sell the dream of musical freedom, music abundance and musical liberty at a low cost (one dollar per song). In doing so, by the same token, they created a need that people did not have at the time!

Very similarly, the Iphone created a need for touch-screen technologies from 2007 while no such equipment existed at the time. Hence, people had no actual need for smartphones because they never thought such tools could exist, but they rapidly became addicted to this technology. Soon after, the need was so big that the competitors had no choice but to launch their versions of the Iphone to match demand.

Of course, the same went for applications that everyone uses today even though we had no need for them ten years ago.

**Needs imply amazement, obsession and dependence.** Shall we continue? Take the Ipad! The logical continuity of the touch-screen revolution!

When those tools came on the market, they amazed the consumer and created the excitation before creating dependence. Geeks started to use them, the cool people eventually followed. Soon after, the idea of owning an Ipad was an obsession for many and, again, led competitors to develop alternative products.

Hence, while tablets did not exist prior to the release of the Ipad, we all use and depend on those tools nowadays to perform simple searches and tasks without a traditional computer or laptop. Talking about laptops, those have largely replaced desktop computers nowadays, thanks perhaps to an increasing reliance on touch screens (a massively attractive Unique Selling Point) and hybrid products like Ipads pro and Microsoft Surface equipment which have transformed novelty into daily.

**Now, how do _you_ create a need?**

Let's challenge you again. How would you defend your leadership strategy with regards to need-creation? Try and answer those questions, think about ways to improve your methods and write your conclusions down.

Do your products answer a need that already exists or have you considered the idea of creating a new need on which you can build upon?

Can you change your customers' lives by creating something they have not thought about yet?

Have you made sure that your product is so great that it will create amazement in the short-term, obsession in the medium-term and eventually dependence in the long-run?

# LEADERSHIP LESSON #6:
# BE AN INNOVATOR

Beyond the idea of motivating, inspiring, creating value and creating needs, an important part of Steve Jobs' leadership consisted in wearing a leader's and innovator's hat. The point is very important, because while this might seem obvious the idea represents a genuine challenge that most C-level leaders and entrepreneurs need to overcome.

**Innovative leadership as a spirit.** Clearly, Steve Jobs had innovative leadership as a motto. His job as a leader was not to manage paperwork, it was to lead the company's innovation and encourage the development of new life-changing tools.

Hence, a major leadership lesson is that while there is only one captain in the boat, that captain has to put himself in the captain's boots and do whatever it takes to become the innovator and leader he needs to become. In other words, stay in your daily routine, you will remain a manager. Work on your innovative leadership skills, and you will be considered as an innovation leader.

**Unleashing creativity.** Now that the captain has decided to wear the captain's boots to be recognized as a leader, he needs to unleash his creativity.

For Steve Jobs, creativity was about being able to create connections between problems, needs and solutions. He would seek inspiration from other industries – including hotel chains – from his travels or even from the calligraphy lessons he took.

For you, creativity could for instance be about creating new types of products seen in very different industries or even abroad, on foreign markets you are absent from but which nonetheless represent an opportunity if a concept can be adapted and imported into your own market.

So, where does your creativity come from?

**Creativity is about taking risks.** Steve Jobs' leadership incorporated the idea (and necessity) to take risks. From both a personal and work perspective.

From a personal perspective, he was convinced that no one can help you better than yourself. He used to say that life is limited in time and would urge people to make the most of their own time. So, he was an advocate of moving forward, would take those risks he deemed necessary to live a life worth living and would follow his own intuition and 'inner voice'.

In a public address, in fact, he said *"Your time is limited, so don't waste it living someone else's life. Don't be trapped by dogma, which is living with the results of other people's thinking. Don't let the noise of others' opinions drown out your own inner voice, heart and intuition. They somehow already know what you truly want to become."*

From a leadership perspective, his approach was very similar. Creativity required taking risks and, as mentioned previously, he took risks when he released products that were to be seen nowhere else at the time, but he somehow also took the risk of jeopardizing his own product line: in making every new innovation better than the previous one, he basically risked making his winning products obsolete!

**Break walls and move on.** This approach to leadership shows that the ability to break walls and move on is essential. In competitive markets where your next move might well be your last move, the ability to take a calculated risk is a game-changer. This ability, however, comes with a very specific mindset, i.e. with the idea that one way or another, leaving an obstacle aside is also about losing an opportunity to do better.

Again, this lesson can be adapted very easily to your own leadership needs. What matters here is to nurture and trust your ability to take a certain – and calculated – amount of risk in order to move forward and explore markets and opportunities that others have not explored yet. Daring is key.

### Are *you* an innovator?

Now, how would you discuss innovation with Steve Jobs if you could?

How would you explain your innovation methods and to what extent would you consider doing things differently?

To what extent is your leadership based on the need to innovate permanently? Are you focusing your daily routine on daily issues or do you actually plan some time off to think about how your company can become recognized as an innovator in your field?

To what extent are you comfortable taking creativity risks?

Do you trust your inner voice and intuition enough when it comes to creation? Or do you only rely on market insights to plan ahead?

What difference would you see if you tried to look forward instead of merely reacting to market transformation as they occur?

Are you ready to disrupt markets and break walls?

# LEADERSHIP LESSON #7:
# SPEAK WELL, SPEAK UP!

The next lesson that can be borrowed from Steve Jobs' leadership is probably the idea that communication is definitely on you too. From the start, you are in charge of setting, following and reviewing your business' goals, as regularly as it takes. But from the start, you are also responsible for making your message to the world loud and clear. Here is a big tip.

**Tell stories!** Steve Job's life tells us a lot about the impact of communication. It shows the importance for a leader to be not only a good communicant but also a performer when it comes to speaking-up.

A key aspect of Jobs' leadership – as discussed earlier in this book – was his ability to sell dreams rather than products to his end-users. Accordingly, this is no surprise that numerous comments and articles online insist on how a fantastic storyteller Jobs was.

Think about it!

Have you watched any presentation or speech by him? Take a look on YouTube, there is a lot to learn from those. Look at the content of the presentations.

Do you see PowerPoints and bullet points? No. What you see is genius storytelling, or the ability to tell the audience a story they will listen, remember and repeat.

Now, I can hear what you think, here is an example. When he launched the first Iphone,

Jobs used a Google Map search to localize a famous coffee shop nearby, then he called it while talking to the audience. The discussion was very brief: "Yes, I'd like to order 4,000 lattes to go, please. [...] No, just kidding. Wrong number. Goodbye!".

Of course, the room enjoyed the play and had a good laugh, but what mattered this day was Jobs' ability not to describe the product but to show how revolutionary it was, by making up a story and, of course, by giving the audience an extraordinary story to tell.

In sum, by telling a story instead of merely presenting pros and cons with bullet points, you can transform a bored audience into an interested audience that will praise your leadership skills and do your marketing for you (and for free) as soon as they leave the room! What else would you need?

**Now, how do _you_ do?**

How do you communicate? Do _you_ communicate or do you let others do that for you because you don't like it and, after all, it's their job?

Can you tell stories? What stories do you tell?

Do you use stories as part of your leadership work to make your company known?

Very honestly, do you tend to hide behind slides and numbers to avoid interacting frankly with people, staffers and clients?

# LEADERSHIP LESSON #8:
# DO THINGS WELL,
# OR DON'T DO THEM

Steve Jobs was a perfectionist and the ability to do things well was inherent to his leadership methods. Let's look at perfection-in-getting-things-done a little closer.

**Don't do things for money.** The starting point when it comes to doing well is – as explained at the beginning of this book – to do things with the right motivations and for the right reasons.

As we've seen earlier, Steve Jobs has always put his vision (bringing computers to every home), the satisfaction of the end-user and the necessity to innovate first. Jobs used to take a $1 annual paycheck and has largely been quoted for saying that he wasn't running the company for money. His shares in the company would largely compensate, of course (no one is expected to work for free), but the point here is to say that one's motivations as a leader must be in line with the vision and the goals.

Don't do things for the money, whatever the amount of your check, do things well because they need to be done well.

**Seek perfection in everything you do.** Steve Jobs was a perfectionist who had an eye for every detail, would seek the best results and would not hesitate to do things again if the results were not up to his expectations.

Steve Jobs for instance had an aversion for imperfect interfaces that could poison user experience while, often, he would be highly upset by the very idea that some applications might ruin the perfection reputation of Apple equipment.

The lesson here, therefore, is that one should always aim for the best. But be careful, Steve Jobs' obsession for perfection did not make unanimity. The quest for excessive perfection can be problematic because better is the enemy of good as we all know.

**Focus for better results.** Following his return to Apple in 1997, Steve Jobs took the decision to review the company's business model and to refocus.

In his opinion, and as reported by his biograph Walter Isaacson, the business model relied on too many products therefore he re-oriented it towards four main segments, including general consumers, professional consumers, desktop products and portable products. Thus, any project falling outside of those categories was considered irrelevant and diverting focus and would therefore be stopped.

Isaacson actually quoted the following remark by Steve Jobs: "Deciding what not to do is as important as deciding what to do". An easy lesson to apply to your own leadership, what do you think?

**Simplify but never compromise on products.** In line with the various ideas discussed previously, Steve Jobs' leadership was also based on the idea that a leader and company should never compromise on products for the sake of making greater profits.

On various online sources, the Apple leader is commonly described as never discussing profit or cost, and as saying that a product's abilities would always make up for its price. Sometimes he would take a product out if its price was deemed too high for the value created for the end-user, but he would not compromise on quality just for the sake of profits.

Steve Jobs was however a strong believer that

simple is better. In other words, the unnecessary is to be eliminated and, as the French Author Antoine de Saint Exupéry said, perfection can only be reached when there is nothing left to take away. So, Jobs used to consider that 'Simplicity is the ultimate sophistication' and built part of his leadership on that very idea. Again, do things well or don't do them at all.

**Now, do _you_ do things well enough?**

Back to you. How would you discuss perfection with Steve Jobs?

From 1 to 7, how much of a perfectionist are you?

Do you believe in perfectionism or would you approach the concept with care?

Again, your motivations matter. Have you sorted them out yet?

Do you think money works as a motivation when it comes to leading a team?

What do you think of perfection?

Can you reach it? Should you reach it? Is better the enemy of good?

Can you differentiate your most efficient tasks and products from the rest? Do you tend to get carried away without knowing what to do?

Have you tried focusing on a niche market?

Have you tried to simplify your product to make it better instead of compromising on quality to make it cheaper?

# LEADERSHIP LESSON #9: HANDLE PEOPLE WITH CARE

Let me start a chapter with a couple of questions, for a change. How do you think people describe your leadership? Are you skilled? Are you instable? Permanently optimistic?

Leadership requires managing people and Steve Jobs' habits on that matter are absolutely worth mentioning here, for better or for worst. On the one hand, his people management methods were focused on achieving excellency. On the other hand, these very same methods never made unanimity and gave Jobs a bad reputation on the matter. As for perfection, the key is therefore to reach a happy medium.

**Manage to keep the best people.** Steve jobs feared what he named 'the Bozo explosion', that is a system in which the failure of the management to seek for the best and get rid of the less efficient only leads to mediocrity.

So, he would ask a lot from his staff and pay them back with honesty at all times. As his biograph reported, Jobs once declared *"if something sucks, I tell people to their face. It's my job to be honest"*. According to publicly available comments, he would also not hesitate to yell at people to see their reactions. When questioned about his leadership, however, he admitted that he could have probably obtained similar results with less pressure, but nonetheless concluded *"But it's not who I am"*.

This means, in other words, that managing people is about being a leader and a diplomat at the same time. To obtain the best from your staff, the art of diplomacy matters.

In reality, is the ability to achieve results at all cost relevant or should we consider that good leaders take care of their staff, back them up and support them, even if it takes a little more time than expected? Steve Jobs' leadership probably teaches us that a happy medium somewhere between would be a great leadership goal.

**'No' must make part of your vocabulary.** It is a no brainer and a very common idea that you will see in many management books and articles all over the place: you must say NO.

It is very simple, those who don't say 'no' will never manage to focus on the important things, the 20% of your time that ought to generate 80% of your income (ever heard of the Pareto Optimum?).

For a variety of reasons, staffers always want to take new initiatives, do new things that excite them. But if those new things fail to serve your business' goals, their time and energy are lost at your expense because money and efforts are diverted uselessly to non-essential tasks!

So, Steve Jobs not only used the word 'no' as a component of his leadership methods, he was also used to making decisions in the best interest of the company.

As he once said, "I'm as proud of what we don't do as I am of what we do." Isaacson, Steve Jobs' biograph, goes even further in analyzing Jobs' approach to saying no and talks about an ability to filter: *"People would come to him with all sorts of problems — legal problems, personnel problems, whatever. And if he didn't want to deal with it, he would not focus on it. He'd give you sort of a blank stare. He would not answer, he wouldn't answer emails... He would pick four or five things that were really important for him to focus on and then just filter out — almost brutally — filter out the rest"* (see the Harvard Business Review article at the end of the book).

This attitude probably had a negative impact on Steve Jobs reputation, but task selection remains a real part of leadership. Find your own method, reach and efficient happy medium and make the most of it.

**Build trust.** In a related manner, managing people requires building a relationship based on trust.

That point is very important, especially if you want to be able to say no. The point here is that building trust allows ensuring that your teams not only follow you but back you up when you decide something. When it comes to saying no, trust will allow them to know that your refusal is not personal for instance, but trust is also essential with regards to project management, career advancement, crisis management, etc.

Of course, building trust is also about managing your customers who, in theory, are people too (right?). For Steve Jobs, trust was about quality and consistency. He would make sure that Apple's new products would always be better than the previous ones and that the end-users would always be both happy and confident enough to buy the next generation of products. Again, trust here comes with reputation and long-term planning.

**Find partners.** That's a key point. As obvious as it sounds, before you can manage people you must find people to manage, starting with business partners.

Partners here does not mean contractors and clients although you clearly need these too. Partners means business associates who will adhere to your vision and help you achieve the goals you set. When he created Apple, Steve Jobs had the support of his friend Steve Wozniak, who helped him building the research and development side of the project! This partnership was fruitful, but it was most likely the most robust pillar of the Apple success story.

There is also the idea of finding team partners, i.e. staff that will help you get things done and will contribute to achieving your goals. We are back to vision here, because team members must have a vision to follow, but it is also your responsibility to make sure that these people are the best (again) and that they are compatible with your leadership values and methods, particularly when it comes to positive-thinking.

Have you ever tried working with negative persons? Of course, we all have… would you do it again? There you go…

**Engage and empower your team.** When he took Apple back, Steve Jobs started organizing empowerment sessions in the form of an exclusive retreat for his top staff where he would launch a massive brainstorming sessions and gather the opinions and thoughts of all his people. The idea there was to make a list of ten priorities based on the team beliefs, but in the end, he would only keep three, thus making them even more important (while keeping a certain form of control over the decision-making process).

Another empowerment method for Steve Jobs consisted in creating opportunities for direct communication. For him, creativity was about spontaneity and face-to-face discussions therefore he had routine weekly team meetings in which he expected people to talk to him, frontally rather than through PowerPoint slides. In his opinion, those who master their topics do not need to hide behind slides, they must confront and defend their ideas, face-to-face.

In other words, there cannot be any strong leadership without staff representation, consideration and empowerment.

A great way to obtain results from your team is to empower them and give them the possibility to do things on their own. First, they will feel considered and respected. Second, they will release you from a daunting decision-making process that will otherwise prevent you from working on more important longer-term issues.

**Now, how do _you_ handle people?**

How do you think people would describe your management?

How do you make sure you actually keep the best and let the less efficient go without creating tensions?

Can you say no?

Are you able to refocus and make decisions when it comes to affecting financial resources to the right projects?

Do people trust your judgment?

Do they actually trust you as a person and as a leader in general? How about partners?

Are you working alone and capable of managing everything on your own?

Do you have a team?

Are you able to engage them?

How can you assess the level of their empowerment?

Is it sufficient to make your company grow and perform better?

# LEADERSHIP LESSON #10:
## WORK ON YOURSELF

A final hack that can be borrowed from Steve Jobs' leadership methods relates to the idea of doing some work on yourself too.

You can have the best vision for your company and business and you can have the best teams surrounding you, but you won't do much if you don't think about yourself a little bit. A couple of clues are worth mentioning here.

**Be yourself, reasonably.** Steve Jobs was true to himself and behaved in a way that reflected his personality. There are obviously limits to this rule, especially when being yourself can harm your reputation and leadership. Otherwise being honest is key.

For this reason, working on yourself is important, if only to determine your style, identify the values you believe in and adapt your leadership to reflect the personality you want people to see and follow. For instance, Steve Jobs was perhaps impatient and direct at times, but he was also known for being passionate and for bringing perfection into his product. The question here, therefore, is who are you and who do you want to be?

**Give failure some credit.** It is often very difficult to accept failure and many tend to take failure as ... failure. That is, without making the most of it.

Failing doesn't matter, what matters is what you learn from it and how you react and build from your learning. In a speech he gave at Stanford, Steve Jobs for instance reflected on his feelings about being fired from Apple. Here is what he said:

*"I didn't see it then, but it turned out that getting fired from Apple was the best thing that could have ever happened to me. The heaviness of being successful was replaced by the lightness of being a beginner again, less sure about everything. It freed me to enter one of the most creative periods of my life."*

The lesson here is... Well, no comments needed, right?

**Kick butts.** Again, forgive my French, but I'm very serious here. We are obviously back to the idea of positive-thinking.

Failure happens all the time. Sometimes you fail at golf or at cooking a chocolate cake, sometimes you fail at school, sometimes you fail with a project, and sometimes you get fired. That's sad for sure but what matters is what you make out of it. What other people say about how you fail means nothing, especially if you can say why your failure has made you stronger.

Everyone fails at some point, Steve Jobs did too, but as the previous quote shows, he was smart enough to transform failure into a form of success that made him look a thoughtful leader. So, kicking butts is important. Live your life, make your own tests, and if people are not happy with what you do or dare commenting on your failures, kick their butt by moving forward when they remain stuck behind! Do, fail, reflect, repeat.

### Now, how do _you_ do?

Discussing those topics with Steve Jobs would have been challenging, but how would you have answered the following questions if he had asked?

Does your leadership image reflect who you are? Are you happy with the perception others have of you?

While being true to yourself is important, have you thought about excesses that could create problems?

How do you deal with success and failures?

Can you handle failure?

Can you handle the way people think about your failures? How do you do that?

Have you ever made a failure a strength?

# HOW ABOUT YOU?
# THINK OVER, NOW!

Now, your turn to think over. The following pages provide a summary of the multiple questions asked throughout this book. Take time to read them again and think. For even greater efficiency, taking a pen and something to write on is a good way to start taking action!

The questions and food for thought are there, it is now up to you to make the most of them!

## What are your motivations?

Are you driven by money, power and results? Is your leadership reflecting your motivations? What room do you leave for passion in your leadership and work methods? To what extent do you manage to motivate and engage your teams and partners and to what extent do you think your motivations help in doing this? Could you achieve more by reviewing your motivations and adapting your leadership to take into account your teams' motivations?

Oh, and of course, have you ever thought about adding a dose of positive-thinking to your leadership style and life?

## What is your vision like?

What is the current state of your niche market and how innovative is your vision?

What will this market be like in two, five or ten years? What innovations will be imposed on your industry? What will your customers expect? Will you create those innovations or will you struggle to follow the innovations or others?

How can you reshuffle the cards to stay on top of the competition and how can you make sure that your team will be there durably to progress with you as new challenges appear? Steve Jobs' answer was clear, he kept anticipating continuously. The vision is on you, your turn now…

## Can you inspire?

Are you in charge? Are you really in charge? Do you take command when it comes to creating the vision and making it happen? Are you occasionally or regularly to leadership issues involving decision-making needs?

If you had to describe yourself, how inspiring would you be? Are you managing your team to achieve numbers and statistics or do you leave room for inspiring and meaningful leadership that allows your staff (and clients) to adhere to your vision, agree to it and make it theirs?

Are you persistent? People always have ideas,

they start new ideas but usually give-up on them very fast. Are you persistent enough to see your ideas become a reality? Do you give-up easily? Are you easily discouraged? Have you considered persisting and insisting more because an idea is worth it?

## Can you create value?

Are you selling products to make cash or do you consider value creation as the core aspect of your business?

How do you describe the value you provide?

Are you selling a dream and helping your end-user to realize something important to him? Is the customer's experience part of the dream you are selling or could that problematic phase of your selling activity become a problem for your customer?

Finally, are you working on building long-term values that will naturally be associated with your brand by the customer and guarantee a steady flow of revenue in the long run?

## Can you create a need?

Do your products answer a need that already exists or have you considered the idea of creating a new need on which you can build upon?

Can you change your customers' lives by creating something they have not thought about yet? Have you made sure that your product is so great that it will create amazement in the short-term, obsession in the medium-term and eventually dependence in the long-run?

## Are you recognized as an innovator?

To what extent is your leadership based on the need to innovate permanently? Are you focusing your daily routine on daily issues or do you actually plan some time off to think about how your company can become recognized as an innovator in your field?

To what extent are you comfortable take creativity risks? Do you trust your inner voice and intuition when it comes to creation or do you only rely on market insights to plan? What difference would you see if you tried to look ahead instead of merely reacting to market transformation as they occur? Are you ready to disrupt and break walls?

## Speak up!

How do you communicate? Do you communicate yourself or do you let others communicate for you? How?

Can you tell stories? Do you use stories as part of your leadership work to make your company known? Honestly, do you tend to hide behind slides and numbers to avoid interacting frankly with people, staffers and clients?

## How well do you do things?

Again, motivations matter.

Have you sorted them out yet? Do you think money works as a motivation when it comes to leading a team?

What do you think of perfection? Can you reach it? Should you reach it? Is better the enemy of good? Do you manage to select between your most efficient tasks and products or do you get carried away without knowing what to do? Have you tried focusing on a niche market? Have you tried to simplify your product to make it better instead of compromising on quality to make it cheaper?

## How do you handle people?

How do you think people would describe your management? How do you make sure you keep the best and let the less efficient go without creating tensions?

Can you say no? Are you able to refocus and make decisions when it comes to affecting financial resources to the right projects?

Do people trust your judgment? Do they actually trust you as a person and as a leader in general? How about partners? Are you working alone and capable of managing everything on your own? Do you have a team? Are you able to engage them? Have you made sure they are empowered enough to make your company grow and perform better?

## How about yourself?

Does your leadership image reflect who you are? Are you happy with the perception others have of you? While being true to yourself is important, have you thought about excesses that could create problems? How do you deal with success and failures? Can you handle failure? Can you handle the way people think about your failures? How do you do that? Have you ever made a failure a strength?

# FURTHER READING

There are numerous comments and articles out there about Steve Jobs and all the information collected for the purpose of writing this book originate from the public domain. Hence, while this book had been drafted with the outmost care, exactness in details cannot be guaranteed.

On Steve Jobs' leadership methods, one article is particularly worth reading: leadership methods, one particular article is particularly worth reading: '*The Real Leadership Lessons of Steve Jobs*' by his biograph Walter Isaacson, as published in the Harvard Business Review in April 2012.

✳ ✳ ✳ ✳

*If you found this book interesting, please consider giving it some nice stars on Amazon!*

*It will only take a second but will have a major impact.* Thank you in advance!

✳ ✳ ✳ ✳

## About 'The Leadership Series'.

The Leadership Series are written with the aim of solving important problems that every single entrepreneur or manager faces one day or another, sooner or later. Only, most people do not seek to address those problems. You apparently are on the way to solving one problem, congratulations!

This book has been edited with the support of Philippe Bonnet, a professional business & leadership coach based in Hong Kong who helps international entrepreneurs based in Asia to deal with their management routine on a daily basis.

The rest will be for you to do!

Take action now!

Made in the USA
Middletown, DE
25 November 2017